TRIBAL TATTOO DESIGNS
FROM THE AMERICAS

Research & concept: Maarten Hesselt van Dinter

Editor: Mark Poysden
Italian: Valeria Scimia
French: Annabel Baltus
German: Lilian Unger
Spanish: Montserrat Sonia Pérez Rodríguez
Design & layout: Inkahootz Amsterdam, www.inkahootz.nl

Also available in the same series by Mundurucu Publishers:
Anche disponibile nella stessa serie di Mundurucu Publishers:
Ainsi disponible dans la même série de Mundurucu Publishers:
In der gleichen Reihe von Mundurucu Publishers ebenfalls erhältlich:
También está disponible en la misma serie de la editorial Mundurucu:

Tribal Tattoo Designs from India
Tribal Tattoo Designs from the Pacific
Tribal Tattoo Designs from Indonesia
Tribal Tattoo Designs from Thailand & Burma

www.mundurucu.com

ISBN-10: 90-810543-0-9
ISBN-13: 978-90-810543-0-0
NUR: 656

Printed in China by SC (sang choy) International Ltd.

Maarten Hesselt van Dinter

TRIBAL TATTOO DESIGNS
FROM THE AMERICAS

MUNDURUCU

PUBLISHERS

CONTENTS

North America

South America

Captions

NORTH AMERICA

Tribal Tattoos from North America

Tattooing was common among the Indian tribes throughout northern America. Women's tattoos were mainly decorations intended to attract the opposite sex. For men, apart from those in West Coast tribes, tattoos symbolised war and conquest. As early as the sixteenth century, the French reported an army of more than 3000 tattooed warriors west of the Great Lakes, led by the chief of the Miami. Most were tattooed with interweaving lines and war symbols such as tomahawks, clubs and arrows. The most extensively tattooed were those from the warlike Iroquois, Huron, Neutral and Tobacco tribes living east of the Great Lakes. The Iroquois, for example, tattooed tribal totems on their chests and symbols indicating the number of enemies they had slain on their thighs.

Warriors of central Plains tribes – the Omaha, Osage, Ponca, Kansa and Quapaw – could select from war symbols, including depictions of bears, clubs, arrows and tomahawks. Only the best Osage warriors could have the 'Honour Packs of War' tattoo on their back and chest. The design consisted of a sacred stone dagger and the tribe's ceremonial pipes. Cree Plains warriors were only permitted tattoos after killing their first enemy. If this took too long, in exceptional circumstances, a warrior could be tattooed if it was foretold in a dream.

Throughout the sub-Arctic region men tattooed their own totem on their chests, hoping that it would strengthen their inner bond with their Manitou, a supernatural power or spirit. Designs included buffalo heads, bears, thunderbirds, horse tracks, suns and stars. On America's north-west coast, Haida, Bellabella and Kwakiutl men and women tattooed their clan symbols on their chest, the front of the thighs, the lower leg and between the shoulder blades. Each design had its own meaning and originated in the totems of the clans into which the tribes were traditionally divided: Bear, Beaver, Wolf or Eagle, or one of the fish families.

Les Tatouages tribaux d'Amérique du nord

L'art du tatouage était répandu chez les tribus indiennes de toute l'Amérique du nord. Pour les femmes il s'agissait principalement de décorations censées attirer le sexe opposé. Pour les hommes, à l'exception des tatouages des tribus de la Côte Ouest, ils étaient des symboles de guerre et de conquête. Dès le seizième siècle, les français ont fait état d'une armée de plus de 3000 guerriers tatoués, à l'ouest des Grands Lacs, avec en tête le chef du Miami. La plupart étaient tatoués de lignes entremêlées, et de symboles de guerre tels que tomahawks, massues et flèches. Les plus tatoués étaient issus des tribus guerrières: Iroquois, Huron, Neutral et Tobbacco habitant à l'est des Grands Lacs. Les Iroquois avaient, par exemple, des totems tribaux tatoués sur leur poitrine, et sur leurs cuisses des symboles indiquant le nombre d'ennemis tués.

Les guerriers des tribus des Plaines centrales –Omaha, Osage, Ponca, Kansa et Quapaw – avaient la possibilité de choisir des symboles de guerre, y compris des représentations d'ours, massues, flèches et tomahawks. Seulement les meilleurs guerriers d'Osage pouvaient avoir leurs honneurs de guerre tatoués sur leur dos et leur poitrine. Le dessin représentait un couteau de pierre sacré et les pipes de cérémonie de la tribu. Les guerriers des Plaines de Cree ne pouvaient être tatoués qu'après avoir tué leur premier ennemi. Si cela prenait trop de temps, un guerrier pouvait être tatoué mais seulement dans des circonstances exceptionnelles et si cela avait été prédit dans un rêve.

Partout dans les régions subarctiques les hommes tatouaient leur propre totem sur leur poitrine, espérant qu'il fortifierait leur lien intérieur avec leur Manitou, pouvoir ou esprit surnaturel. Les dessins représentaient des têtes de buffle, des ours, des thunderbirds ou oiseaux tonnerre, des pistes de chevaux, des soleils et des étoiles. Sur la côte nord-ouest de l'Amérique, chez les Haida, les hommes et les femmes de Bella Bella et de Kwakiutl avaient les symboles de leur clan tatoués sur leur poitrine, la partie supérieure des cuisses, le bas de la jambe et entre les omoplates. Chaque dessin avait une signification lui étant propre et trouvait son origine dans les totems des clans dans lesquels les tribus ont été traditionnellement divisées: L'ours, le Castor, le Loup ou l'Aigle, ou une des familles de poisson.

Stammes-Tätowierungen in Nordamerika

Bei den Indianerstämmen in ganz Nordamerika war das Tätowieren üblich. Für die Frauen waren die Tätowierungen hauptsächlich Dekorationen, die darauf abzielten das andere Geschlecht anzuziehen. Für die Männer, mit Ausnahme der Stämme der Westküste, stellten sie Symbole des Krieges und der Eroberung dar. Bereits im sechzehnten Jahrhundert berichteten die Franzosen von einer Armee von mehr als 3000 tätowierten Kriegern westlich der Großen Seen, die durch das Stammesoberhaupt von Miami angeführt wurden. Die meisten waren mit in sich verflochtenen Linien und Kriegssymbolen wie zum Beispiel Tomahawks, Totschlägern und Pfeilen tätowiert. Am umfangreichsten tätowiert waren die der kriegerischen Irokesen, Huronen, Neutralen-und Tabakstämme, die östlich der Großen Seen lebten. Die Irokesen, zum Beispiel, trugen Stammestotems auf ihrer Brust und Symbole an ihren Schenkeln, die die Anzahl der von ihnen erschlagenen Feinde erkennen ließen.

Krieger zentraler Präriestämme – die, der Omaha, Osage, Ponca, Kansa und Quapaw – konnten aus Kriegessymbolen, darunter Darstellungen von Bären, Klubs, Pfeilen und Tomahawks wählen. Nur die besten Osage Krieger trugen die „Ehrenmeute des Krieges" Tätowierung auf Rücken und Brust. Der Entwurf bestand aus dem Messer eines heiligen Steines und der zeremoniellen Pfeife des Stammes. Den Prärie-Cree Kriegern waren Tätowierungen erst nach der Tötung ihres ersten Feindes erlaubt. Wenn dies zu lang dauerte, konnte ein Krieger unter außergewöhnlichen Umständen tätowiert werden, wenn es ihn in einem Traum vorhergesagt wurde.

In der gesamten sub-arktischen Region tätowierten Männer ihren eigenen Totem auf ihre Brust in der Hoffnung, dadurch ihre innere Verbindung mit ihrem Manitu, einer übernatürlichen Kraft oder Geistes stärken würde. Die Entwürfe umfassten Büffelköpfe, Bären, Donnervögel, Pferdespuren, Sonnen und Sterne. An der Nordwestküste Amerikas, bei den Haida, Bellabella und der Kwakiutl, trugen Männer und Frauen ihre Clan-Symbole auf ihrer Brust, der Vorderseite der Schenkel, dem Unterschenkel und zwischen den Schulternblättern. Jeder Entwurf hatte seine eigene Bedeutung und ging aus den Totems der Clans hervor, in den die Stämme traditionell geteilt wurden: Bär, Biber, Wolf oder Adler, oder einem der Fisch-Arten.

Tatuaggi Tribali del Nord America

Tra le tribú Indiane di tutto il Nord America il tatuaggio era cosa commune. Per le donne erano soprattutto una decorazione intesa ad attrarre il sesso opposto. Per gli uomini, tranne quelli delle tribú della Costa Ovest, i tatuaggi erano simboli di guerra e conquista. Già nel sedicesimo secolo, i Francesi registrarono ad ovest dei Grandi Laghi un esercito di oltre 3000 guerrieri tatuati, condotti dal capo dei Miami. La maggior parte erano tatuati con linee intrecciate e simboli di guerra come tomahawks, mazze e freccie. Quelli maggiormente tatuati provenivano dalle bellicose tribú degli Irochesi, Huron, Neutrali e Tobacco che vivevano ad est dei Grandi Laghi. Gli Irochesi, per esempio, si tatuavano totem tribali sul petto e, sulle cosce, simboli che indicavano il numero di nemici uccisi.

I guerrieri delle tribú delle Pianure Centrali – gli Omaha, gli Osage, i Ponca, i Kansa e i Quapaw – potevano scegliere fra vari simboli di guerra, incluse raffigurazioni di orsi, mazze, freccie e tomahawks. Solo i migliori guerrieri Osage potevano avere tatuati gli 'Onori di Guerra' sui loro petti e sulle loro schiene. Il disegno consisteva nel coltello di pietra sacra e pipe cerimoniali della tribú. Ai guerrieri delle pianure Cree era concesso tatuarsi solo dopo aver ucciso il loro primo nemico. Se ciò impiegava troppo tempo, in circostanze eccezionali, un guerriero poteva venir tatuato, se questo fosse stato predetto in un sogno.

Attraverso la regione sub-Artica gli uomini si tatuavano i propri totem sul petto, sperando che questo rafforzasse il loro legame interno con il loro Manitou, un potere o spirito soprannaturale. I disegni includevano teste di bufalo, orsi, Uccelli di Tuono, impronte di cavallo, soli e stelle. Sulla costa nordovest Americana, tra gli Haida, i Bellabella e i Kwakiutl gli uomini e le donne avevano i simboli del loro clan tatuati sul petto, sul davanti delle cosce, sulla parte bassa delle gambe e fra le scapole. Ogni disegno aveva un significato proprio e proveniva dal totem del clan secondo cui le tribú erano tradizionalmente divise: Orso, Castoro, Lupo o Aquila, o una delle specie ittiche.

Los tatuajes tribales de Norteamérica

En toda Norteamérica, era muy común el uso de los tatuajes entre las tribus indígenas. Las mujeres lo utilizaban como medio de seducción para el sexo opuesto. Sin embargo, para los hombres, a excepción de aquellos pertenecientes a las tribus de Costa del Oeste, era un símbolo guerrero y de sus conquistas. A principios del siglo XVI, los franceses fueron informados de un ejército con más de 3000 tatuajes al oeste. Los guerreros de Los Grandes Lagos, dirigido por el jefe de Miami. La mayoría de ellos fueron tatuados con diseños de símbolos de guerras, tales como: hachas, flechas, palos etc. La mayoría de estos tatuajes procedían de Iroqués, Hurón, Neutral y las tribus de Tabaco, que vivían al este de Los Grandes Lagos. Un ejemplo del tatuaje Iroqués eran los totems tribales en los pechos y, a su vez, los símbolos que indicaban el número de enemigos que ellos habían matado se los tatuaban en los muslos. Los guerreros de tribus centrales de las Llanuras: El Omaha, Osage, Ponca, Kansa y Quapaw, podían escoger entre diferentes símbolos de guerra, incluso tatuajes de osos, los palos, las flechas y las hachas de guerra antes mencionadas. Algo muy peculiar, era que sólo los mejores guerreros tenían el privilegio de poder llevar tatuados el denominado " Paquete de Honor de guerra", esto significaba llevar un tatuaje en la espalda y en el pecho. El diseño de dicho tatuaje, consistía en el dibujo de un cuchillo sagrado de piedra y los tubos ceremoniales de tribu. Los guerreros de las llanuras de Cree permitían los tatuajes, sólo después de matar a su primer enemigo. Si ésto tomaba mucho tiempo, se permitía tatuar a un guerrero si se había predecido en los sueños.

Otra singularidad, es que a través de los hombres subárticos de la región tatuaban su propio tótem en el pecho. De esta manera, esperaban reforzar su lazo interno con su Manitou, que era un poder o espíritu sobrenatural. Entre los diseños para estos tatuajes incluían cabezas de búfalo, osos, pájaros de trueno, los vestigios de caballos, soles y estrellas.

En la costa del Noroeste de América, entre el Haida, Bellabella y hombres de Kwakiutk y sus mujeres tenían símbolos del propio clan tatuados tanto en el cuello, como en la parta frontal de los muslos, en las pantorrillas y tambíén entre los omoplatos. Por supuesto, cada diseño tuvo su propio significado y originó una separación tradicional, entre las tribus de los tótems de los ÿclanes: El oso, el castor el lobo o el águila y alguna criatura de la familia de los peces.

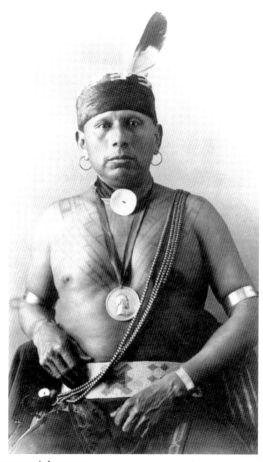

13

Osage
Warrior with ceremonial tattoos

14

Mandan
Chief with war symbols

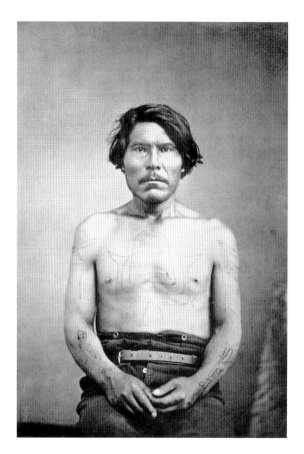

15

Haida
Man with chest and arm tattoos

Arapaho
Chief Black Coyote

Mohawk
Chief Sa Ga Yeath Qua Pieth Tow

18

Haida
Man with chest and arm tattoos

Minatari
Tattooed warrior

Kutchin
Warrior with facial tattoos

Dakota
Tattooed warrior

Cree
Tattooed chief

23

Timuca
Chiefs

Sioux
Warrior

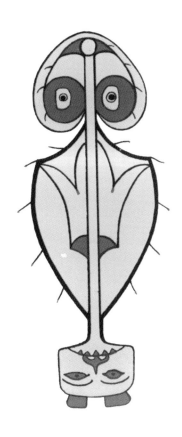

Haida
Halibut

Haida
Double Thunderbird

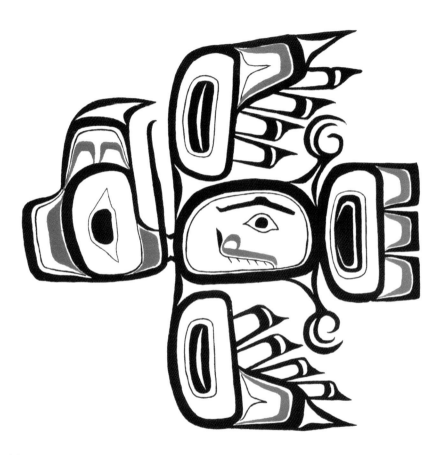

Haida
Fish Eagle

Haida
Whales Head

Inuit
Poster advertising the display of a tattooed Eskimo woman with her child in 1566

Chinook
Tattooed woman with modified head

Wichita
Tattooed woman

32

Naskapi
Woman with Christian cross tattoo

Mohave
Tattooed woman

Inuit
Tattooed women

Ponca
Tattooed girl

Louisiana
Sunpriest

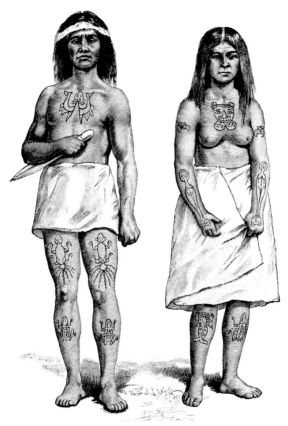

Haida
Tattooed couple
front

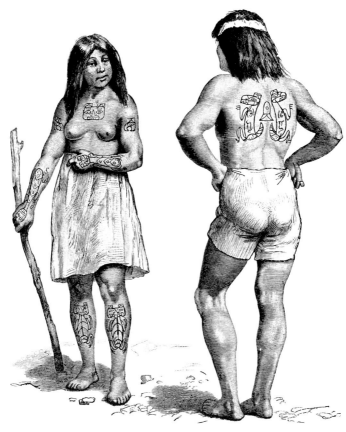

Haida
Tattooed couple
back

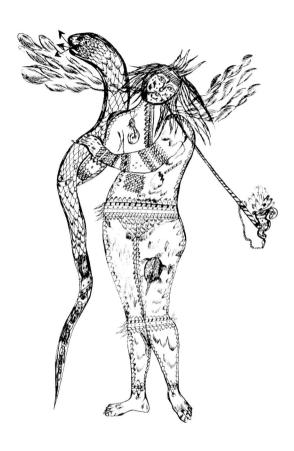

Iroqois
Tattooed warrior

Osage
Warrior with war symbols

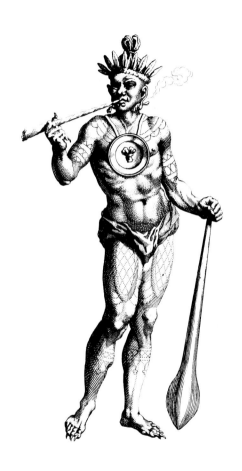

Florida
Tattooed warrior

Creek
Warrior with chest tattoo

Haida
Thunderbird

44

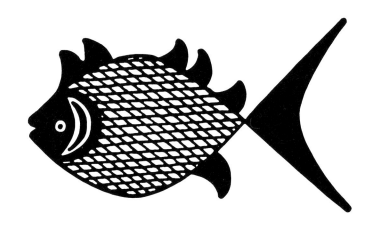

Mimbres
Fish

Mimbres
Fish

Manatee

Mimbres
Turtle

48

Bird motif

Cree
Buffalo That Walks Like a Man

Bird motif

SW America
Spiral bird motif

52

SW America
Spiral motif

53

NW Coast
Hocker design

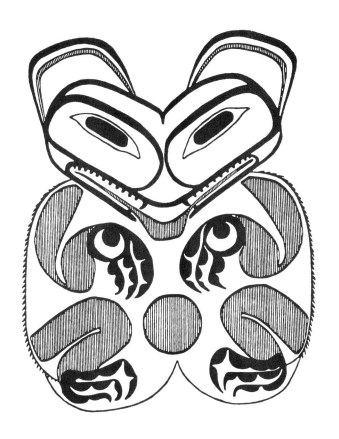

Tsimshian
Bear

Haida
Bear

Haida
Bear

Haida
Bear

Haida
Bear cub

Haida
Wasgo (Sea-Wolf)

Haida
Double Wasgo (Sea-Wolf)

Haida
Killer Whale

NW Coast
Double Killer Whale

Kwakiutl
Killer Whale

Haida
Orca

Kwakiutl
Whale

Haida
Fabulous Sea Monster

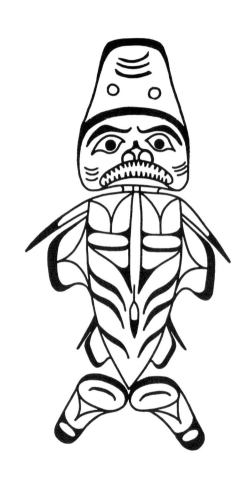

Haida
Dogfish

Haida
Squid

69

Haida
Sculpin

70

Haida
Sculpin

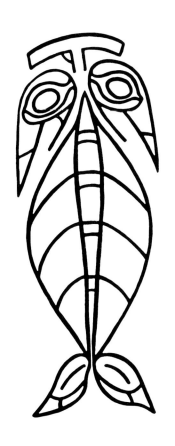

Haida
Sculpin

Haida
Sculpin

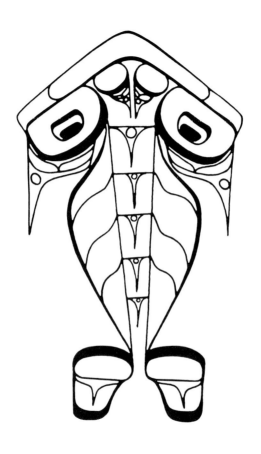

Haida
Sculpin

74

Haida
Cod

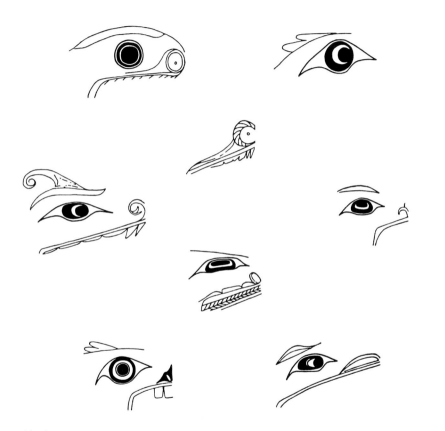

Kwakiutl
Eyes

Kwakiutl
Wing and fin designs

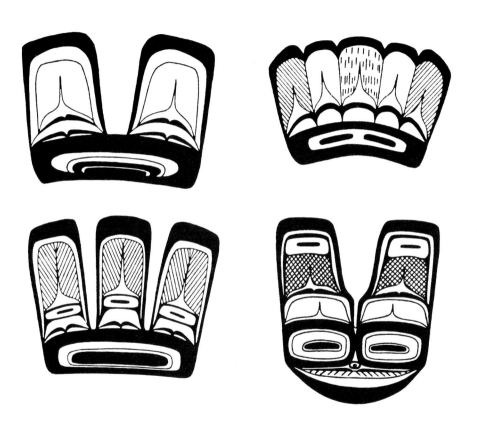

Kwakiutl
Wing and fin designs

Kwakiutl
Thunderbird

Tlingit
Thunderbird

Kwakiutl
Thunderbird

Haida
Thunderbird

NW America
Eagle

83

Kwakiutl
Thunderbird

Kwakiutl
Raven

Haida
Double Thunderbird

Haida
Duck

Haida
Double Raven

Haida
Raven

Haida
Crow

Haida
Double Raven

Kwakiutl
Raven

Haida
Mythic Raven

Haida
Dragonfly

Tsimshian
Dragonfly

Haida
Hawk-moth

Haida
Frog

Haida
Grizzly Bear

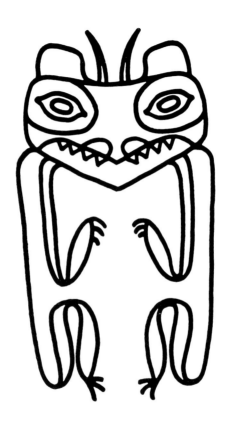

Haida
Mountain Goat

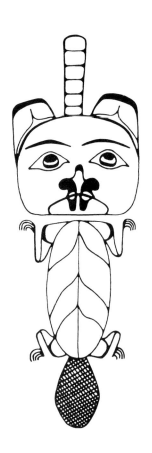

Haida
Beaver

Kwakiutl
Beaver

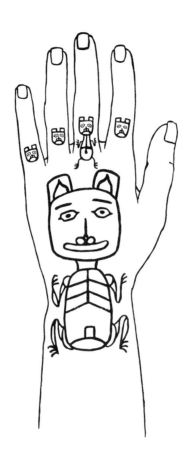

Haida
Bear and tshimo's

Haida
Thunderbird and tshimo's

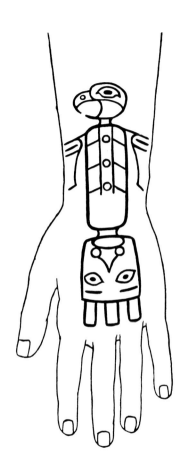

Haida
Thunderbird

104

Haida
Thunderbird

Haida
Double Wolf

Haida
Bear bracelet

Haida
Sea Monster bracelet

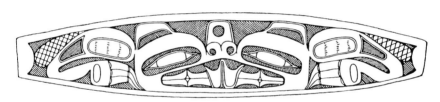

Haida
Beaver bracelet

Kwakiutl
Hawk

Tsimshian
Sea Monster

Kwakiutl
Sisiutl (snake spirit)

Georgia
Anthropomorhished Serpent

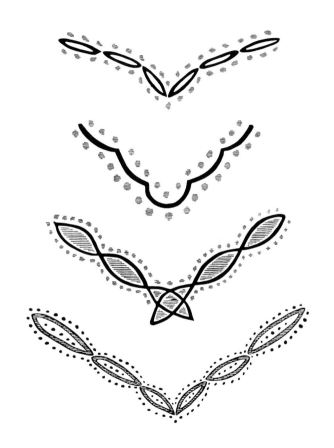

Mohegan
Back designs

114

Osage
Chest tattoo

115

Cree
Grizzly Bear

116

Cree
Rattlesnake and Buffalo Spirit

Cree
Baby Thunderbird

Cree
Manito

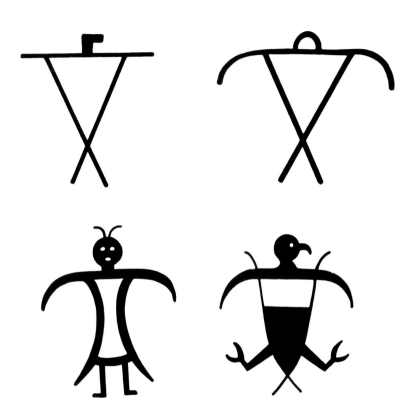

Plains Cree
Thunderbirds

Ojibwa
Thunderbird

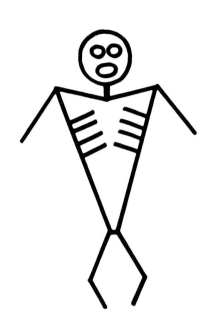

Ojibwa
Skeleton and Otter Man

122

Thompson
Tattoo designs

Yavapai
Tattoo designs

Plains
Geometrical designs

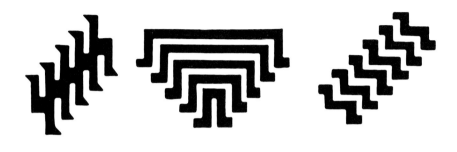

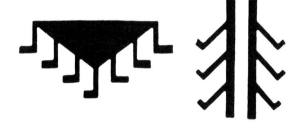

Yuki
Quill Tip designs

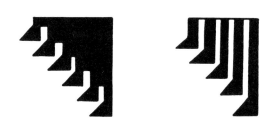

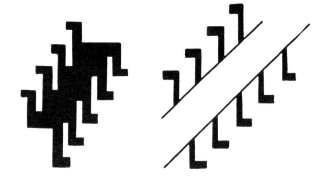

Yuki
Quill Tip designs

Mimbres
Geometrical designs

128

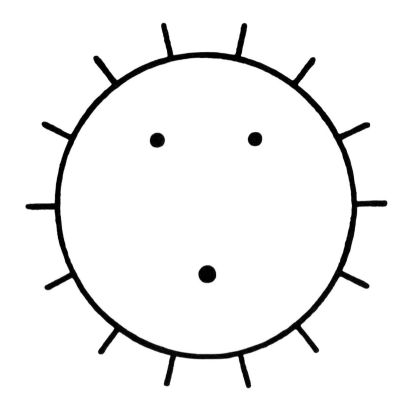

Kwakiutl
Sun

129

Inuit
Serpent

SW America
Squash blossom

SW America
Swastika

132

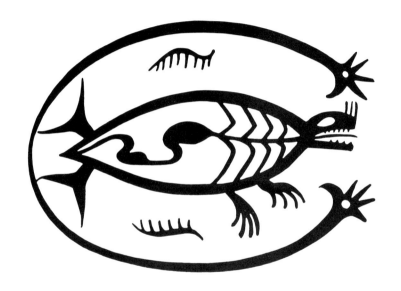

Inuit
Seal and serpent

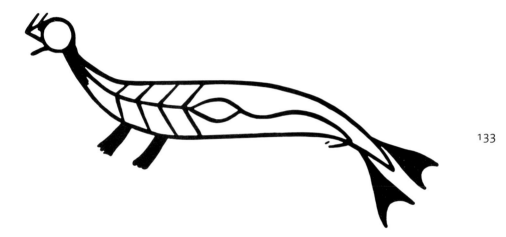

133

Inuit
Seal

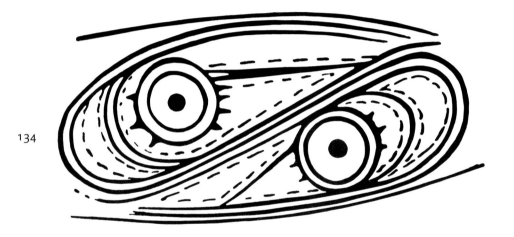

Inuit
Traditional tattoo design

135

Arkansas
Horned Snake

Haida
Wolf

Alabama
Winged Snake

SOUTH AMERICA

Tribal Tattoos from South America

Among the Maya and other indigenous Mexican peoples, it was customary for tattoos to be applied as decorations for bravery in war. The Spanish observed these tattoos on the Zapotec, Huaxtec Totonac Itza and Maya. The designs, usually on the chest and thighs, were glyphs and stylised apes, tigers, snakes, eagles and other birds. The number of images indicated a warrior's status. A young warrior would begin with one or two symbolic figures, adding a design for each victim. An old warrior could thus be completely covered with the evidence of his glorious past. Itza warriors also decorated their faces with an image of the animal that represented either a man's totem or his family spirit. For the Maya, facial tattoos were taboo, though decorations on pre-Colombian pots and figurines suggest that this had not always been the case. It is also known that Maya nobility caught stealing were punished by being publicly tattooed from the chin to the ear. Aztec and Maya people were named after the day-sign on which they were born. It was not unusual for these names to be painted or tattooed on their hands and arms.

In Peru, a 1500-year-old mummy has been discovered of a girl with hair two metres long and a tattoo of a bird on her left arm. Inca tattoos generally consisted of geometric motifs and abstract depictions of everyday objects, heavenly bodies and animals. Stylised millipedes, fish and birds were especially common. Pots and vases excavated along the west coast of South America are decorated with zigzag lines, lozenges and stylised depictions of animals such as snakes, birds, fish and mythical creatures. If these were used as tattoos, it suggests that even older tribes such as the Nazca, Moche and Chimu were familiar with the practice.

In the Amazon jungle, warriors from the cannibalistic Tupinamba and the fearsome Mundurucu protected themselves against evil spirits by tattooing a 'suit of armour' over their bodies. The shaman or medicine man from the tribe scratched parallel lines over the whole body with a 'wound scratcher', a saw made with the teeth of a wild animal.

Les Tatouages tribaux d'Amérique du sud

Chez les Mayas et autres peuplades mexicaines indigènes, il était coutume d'appliquer des tatouages en signe de bravoure de guerre. Les espagnols ont observé ces tatouages chez les Zapotec, Huaxtec Totonac Itza et Maya. Les dessins, en général sur la poitrine et les cuisses, étaient des glyphes, et des singes, des tigres, des serpents, des aigles et d'autres oiseaux stylisés. Le nombre d'images indiquait le statut du guerrier. Un jeune guerrier commençait avec une ou deux figures symboliques, et ajoutait une figure à chaque victime. Un vieux guerrier pouvait ainsi être complètement recouvert de son glorieux passé. Les guerriers d'Itza ont aussi décoré leur visage de l'animal qui représentait soit le totem de l'homme soit l'esprit de sa famille. Pour les Mayas, les tatouages du visage étaient tabous, bien que les décorations sur les pots et les figurines précolombiennes suggèrent que ceci n'ait pas toujours été le cas. Il est aussi connu que la noblesse maya surprise en train de voler était punie publiquement d'un tatouage allant du menton à l'oreille. Les peuples Aztèque et Maya étaient nommés d'après le signe du jour ou ils étaient nés. Il n'était pas rare que ces noms soient peints ou tatoués sur leurs mains et leurs bras.

Au Pérou, une momie vieille de 1500 ans a été découverte, il s'agit d'une fille avec des cheveux de deux mètres de long et un tatouage d'oiseau sur le bras gauche. Les tatouages incas formaient généralement des motifs géométriques et des représentations abstraites d'objets de tous les jours, des corps et des animaux célestes. Les plus répandus étaient des mille-pattes, des poissons et oiseaux stylisés. Sur la côte Ouest de l'Amérique du sud, des pots et des vases ont été mis à jour, décorés de lignes en zigzag, de losanges et de représentations stylisées d'animaux tels que serpents, oiseaux, poissons, et créatures mythiques. Si ceux-ci ont été utilisés comme tatouages, cela suggère que même les plus anciennes tribus telles que Nazca, Moche et Chimu connaissaient cette pratique.

Dans la jungle amazonienne, les guerriers du cannibale Tupinamba et le redoutable Mundurucu se protégeaient des esprits diaboliques en tatouant une « armure » sur leur corps. Le chamane ou sorcier guérisseur de la tribu griffait des lignes parallèles sur tout le corps avec un 'gratteur à blessure', une scie faite avec les dents d'un animal sauvage.

Stammes-Tätowierungen in Südamerika

Bei den Maya und anderen eingeborenen mexikanischen Völkern war es üblich, dass Tätowierungen als Auszeichnungen für Tapferkeit im Krieg angewandt wurden. Die Spanier haben diese Tätowierungen bei den Zapoteken, Huaxteken Totonaken, Itzá und Maya beobachtet. Die Entwürfe, gewöhnlich auf Brust und Schenkel, waren Zeichen und stilisierte Affen, Tiger, Schlangen, Adler und andere Vögel. Die Anzahl der Abbildungen gab den Status eines Kriegers zu erkennen. Ein junger Krieger begann mit der ein oder anderen symbolischen Figur, ein Bildnis für jedes Opfer hinzuzufügend. Ein alter Krieger konnte entsprechend vollständig mit dem Beweis seiner ruhmreichen Vergangenheit bedeckt sein. Itzá Krieger haben auch ihre Gesichter mit dem Bildnis eines Tieres geschmückt, dass entweder den Totem eines Mannes oder seinen Familiengeist repräsentierte. Für die Maya waren Gesichts-Tätowierungen tabu, obwohl Dekorationen auf prä-kolumbianischen Töpfen und Statuetten nahe legen, dass dies nicht immer der Fall war. Es ist ebenfalls bekannt, dass man Adlige der Maja, die man beim Stehlen ertappte, bestrafte, in dem sie öffentlich vom Kinn bis zum Ohr tätowiert wurden. Die Azteken und Maya wurden nach dem Tageszeichen benannt, an dem sie geboren wurden. Es war nicht ungewöhnlich, dass diese Namen auf Hände und Arme gemalt oder tätowiert wurden.

In Peru ist die 1500 Jahre alte Mumie eines Mädchens mit zwei Meter langen Haaren und der Tätowierung eines Vogels auf ihrem linken Arm entdeckt worden. Inka Tätowierungen bestanden gewöhnlich aus geometrischen Motiven und abstrakten Darstellungen alltäglicher Objekte, Himmelskörper und Tieren. Stilisierte Tausendfüßler, Fische und Vögel waren besonders verbreitet. An der Westküste Südamerikas wurden Töpfe und Vasen ausgegraben, die mit Zickzack-Linien, Rauten und stilisierten Darstellungen von Tieren wie beispielsweise   Schlangen, Vögeln, Fischen und Fabeltieren verziert waren. Sofern diese als Tätowierungen verwendet wurden, lässt dies vermuten, dass sogar ältere Stämme wie zum Beispiel die Nazca, die Moche und die Chimú vertraut waren mit dieser Praxis.

Im Dschungel des Amazonas haben sich Krieger der kannibalischen Tupinamba und der furchterregenden Munduruku gegen böse Geister geschützt, in dem sie sich eine Rüstung auf den Körper tätowierten. Der Schamane oder Medizinmann des Stammes kratzte mit Hilfe eines „Wunden-Kratzers"- einer Säge, hergestellt aus den Zähnen wilder Tiere-parallele Linien auf den gesamten Körper.

Tatuaggi Tribali del Sud America

Fra i Maya ed altre popolazioni indigene Messicane, era consueto l'utilizzo di tatuaggi come decorazioni di coraggio in guerra. Gli Spagnoli notarono questi tatuaggi sugli Zapotechi, Huastechi, Totonachi, Itza e Maya. I disegni, solitamente sul petto e cosce, rappresentavano simboli e scimmie, tigri, serpenti, aquile e altri uccelli stilizzati. Il numero di immagini indicava il rango di un soldato. Un cavaliere giovane avrebbe iniziato con una o due figure simboliche, e aggiunto un disegno per ogni vittima. Un guerriero adulto poteva quindi essere completamente ricoperto con l'evidenza del suo passato glorioso. I guerrieri Itza, inoltre, si decoravano le facce con l'immagine dell'animale che rappresentava il loro totem o lo spirito della loro famiglia. Per i Maya, i tatuaggi sul viso erano taboo, sebbene decorazioni su ceramiche e statuette pre-Colombiane suggeriscono che ciò non sia stato sempre cosí. È anche risaputo che la punizione per i nobili Maya sorpresi a rubare era venir tatuati da mento a orecchio pubblicamente. I Maya e gli Aztechi portavano i nomi del segno del giorno in cui erano nati. Non era insolito che questi nomi venissero dipinti o tatuati sulle loro braccia e mani.

In Perú è stata scoperta, dopo 1500 anni, una mummia di una ragazza con i capelli lunghi due metri ed il tatuaggio di un uccello sul braccio sinistro. I tatuaggi inca consistevano generalmente di motivi geometrici e rappresentazioni astratte di utensili, divinità e animali. Millepiedi, pesci e uccelli stilizzati erano specialmente comuni. Sulla costa ovest del Sud America, sono stati ritrovati vasi e contenitori decorati con linee a zigzag, losanghe e raffigurazioni stilizzate di animali come serpenti, uccelli, pesci e creature mitologiche. Se tali disegni venivano usati anche nei tatuaggi, ciò indicherebbe che anche tribú piú antiche come i Nazca, Moche e Chimu avevano familiarità con questa pratica.

Nella foresta Amazzonica i guerrieri dei cannibali Tupinamba e dei temuti Mundurucu si proteggevano contro gli spiriti maligni tatuandosi un' "armatura" di linee sul proprio corpo. Lo sciamano, o medico della tribú, si graffiava una "veste" di linee parallele su tutto il corpo con un "rastrello da ferita", una sega fatta di denti di animale selvaggio.

Tatuajes tribales de Sudamérica

Entre los mayas y otros indíndigenas méxicanos era costubre utilizar los tatujes como símbolos y decoraciones como representación del valor en las guerras. Los españoles observaron dichos tatuajes en las tribus Zapotec, Huaxtec otonac Itza y Maya. Los diseños de los tatuajes estaban basados en dibujos de animales tales como: monos estilizados, tigre, serpientes y águilas entre otras aves. El número de tatuajes indicaba la posición que poseía el guerrero. De esta forma, un guerrero jóven empezaría con uno o con dos figuras simbólicas, agregando un diseño para cada víctima. Un guerrero mayor podía estar cubierto completamente con la evidencia de su pasado glorioso. Los guerreros de Itza hacían uso de los tatuajes grabando también sus caras con la imagen del animal que representaba o un tótem de un hombre o espíritu de familia. Esta era una diferencia con respecto a los Mayas, para los cuales el tatuaje facial era tabú. Sin embargo, he de añadir que en algunas decoraciones en ollas y firillas precolombias sugieren que éste no siempre había sido el caso. Por otro lado, una manera muy peculiar de castigar a los ladrones en la cultura Maya consistía en tatuarlos desde el mentón hasta la oreja, publicamente y por los miembros de la nobleza. Los Aztecas y los Mayas eran nombrados con el símbolo correspondiente después de su nacimiento. No era algo excepcional que estos nombres fuesen pintados o tatuados tanto en las manos como en los armamentos.

En Perú, una momia de 1500 años de edad fue descubierta. La momia era de una chica con un cabello que medía dos metros de largo y llevaba un tatuaje de un pájaro en el brazo izquierdo. Los tatuajes de los Incas consistían generalmente en figuras geométricas y algunas descripiciones abstractas de los utensilios diarios, así como de los cuerpos celestes y también animales. Entre los más comunes destacan: los milpiés estilizados, el pez y las aves. Una característica de la costa occidental de Sudamérica, es que en las ollas y en los jarrones que se han encontrado durante las excavaciones, han sido decorados con líneas en zig-zag, las pastillas y descripciones estilizadas de animales como serpientes, aves, peces y otras criaturas míticas. Podemos hacernos a la idea pues, de que si éstos se utilizaron como tatuajes, en dichas tribus, hace suponer que las tribus mas antiguas como por ejemplo la Nazca, Moche y Chimu conocían ya la práctica.

En la selva Amazona, los guerreros del Tupinamba canibalista y el Mundurucu terrible se protegían a sí mismos contra los malos espíritus tatuando " el juicio de blindaje" sobre sus cuerpos. El Chamán o el curandero de la tribu se tatuaba sobre el cuerpo entero con una " herida-arañada" hecha con los dientes de un animal salvaje.

Mexico
Mask with facial tattoo designs

Peru
Nazca
Figurine with tattoo designs

147

Peru
Nazca
Figurine with tattoo designs

Costa Rica
Anthropomorphic pottery with tattoo designs

Peru
Inca
Anthropomorphic pottery with facial tattoo designs

Mexico
Aztec
Sun Sacrifice

Brasil
Mundurucu

152

Mexico
Aztec
Eagle

153

Mexico
Aztec
Eagle

Mexico
Aztec
Eagle

Mexico
Aztec
Ocomatli (ape god)

156

Mexico
Maya

157

Mexico
Aztec
Mictlantecuhtli (god of the dead)

Mexico
Aztec
Hallucinogenic plant

159

Mexico
Aztec
Jaguar

Peru
Moche
Anthropomorphic pottery with facial tattoo designs.

Colombia
Figurine with tattoo designs

162

Brasil
Mundurucu

163

Brasil
Mundurucu
Woundscratcher

FRANCOIS CARYPYRA.

164

Brasil
Tupinamba

Mexico
Aztec
Quetzalcoatl (Feathered Serpent)

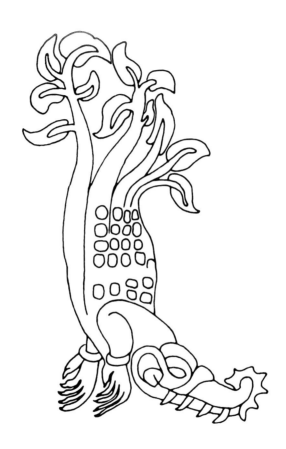

166

Mexico
Aztec
Crocodile tree

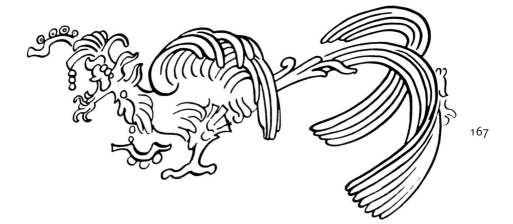

167

Mexico
Sacred Quetzal Bird

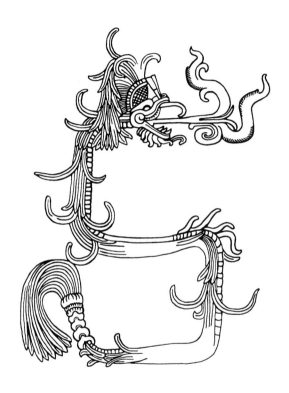

Mexico
Quetzalcoatl (Plumed Serpent)

169

Mexico
Aztec
Tiger fighting eagle

Mexico
The divine serpent Kukulkan

Mexico
Quetzalcoatl as Wind God

172

Peru
Moche
Centipede

173

Mexico
Eagle

174

Mexico
Toltec
Eagle

175

Mexico
Aztec
Eagle

176

Mexico
Toltec
Vulture

177

Mexico
Teotihuacan
Solar eagle

Mexico
Solar eagle devouring human hearts

Mexico
Aztec
Hieroglyph of the Burning Water

Mexico
Aztec
Skull

Mexico
Monster

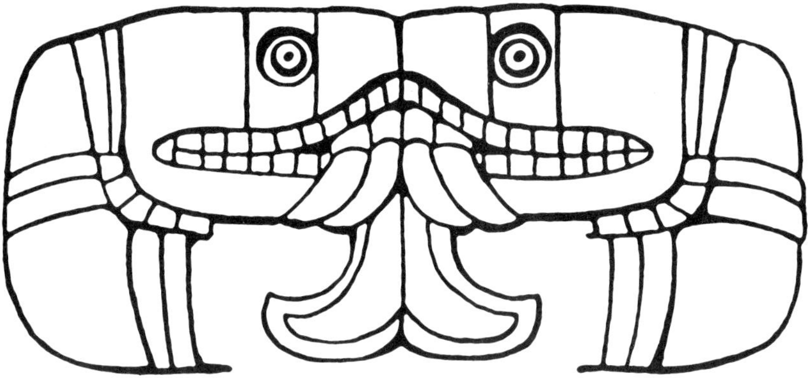

Mexico
Aztec
Coatlicue (Earth goddess)

183

Mexico
Teotihuacan
Tiger Bird Serpent

Mexico
Teotihuacan
Face symbolizing the Fifth Sun

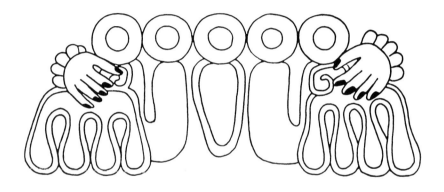

Mexico
Nauatl
The Hand of God

Mexico
Teotihuacan
The Hand of God

187

Mexico
Teotihuacan
Butterflies

188

Mexico
Maya
Suns & stars

189

Mexico
Teotihuacan
Tiny animals

190

Mexico
Olmec
Dragon

Mexico
Olmec
Dragon

192

Peru
Moche
Crabman

Peru
Moche
Anthropomorphised crab

Peru
Moche
Iguana

Mexico
Teotihuacan
Quetzalcoatl as the Lord of Dawn

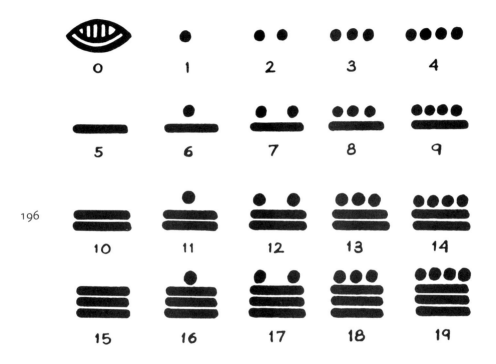

Mexico
Maya
Numbers

Kin (1 day)

Uinal (1 month)

Tun (1 year)

Katun (20 yeas)

Maya
Period signs

pop   uo   zip   zotz   tzec

xul   yaxkin   mol   chen   yax

zac   ceh   mac   kankin   muan

pax   kayab   cumku   uayeb

Mexico
Maya
Month signs (solar year)

mix   ik   akbal   kan   chicchan

cimi   manik   lamat   muluk   oc

chuen   eb   ben   ix   men

cib   caban   eznab   cauac   ahau

Mexico
Maya
Day signs

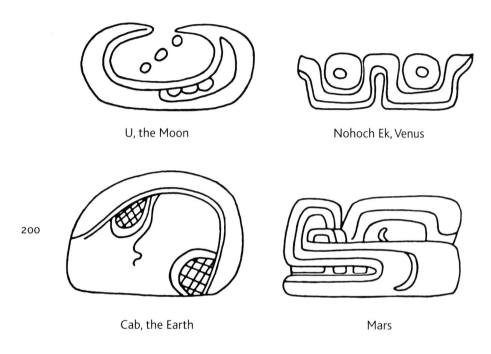

U, the Moon

Nohoch Ek, Venus

Cab, the Earth

Mars

Mexico
Maya
Signs for the heavenly bodies

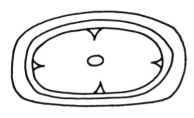

Kin, the Sun

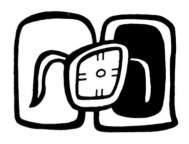

Solar eclipse

Caan, the sky

Mexico
Maya
Signs for the heavenly bodies

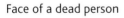

Face of a dead person

Maggot

Mexico
Maya
Death glyphs

203

Mexico
Aztec
Spiderwater (orchid)

204

Mexico
Serpent

Mexico
Aztec
Bird motif

Peru
Jaguar

207

Mexico
Aztec
Hockers

208

Mexico
Aztec
Hockers

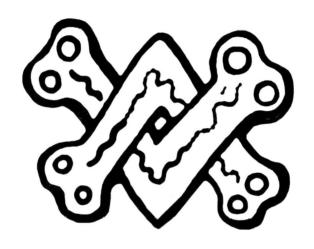

Mexico
Maya
Death symbol

Mexico
Aztec
Pierced heart

211

Mexico
Aztec
Pierced heart

Mexico
Cross of Quetzalcoatl

213

Mexico
Maya
Hieroglyph of Venus

214

Mexico
Aztec
Symbols of movement

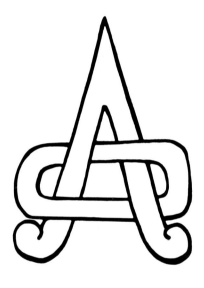

Mexico
Year symbol

216

Mexico
Zapotec
Hieroglyph of the Morning Star

Gold

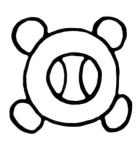

Turquoise

Mosaic

Jade

Obsidian

Mexico
Aztec
Hieroglyps for precious stones

Cipactli (crocodile)

Ehecatl (wind)

Calli (house)

Cuetzpallin (lizard)

Coatl (snake)

218

Mexico
Aztec
Day signs

Miquiztli (death)

Mazatl (deer)

Atl (water)

Tochctli (rabbit)

Itzquintli (dog)

219

Mexico
Aztec
Day signs

Ocelotl (jaguar)

Cuautli (eagle)

220

Ozomatli (monkey)

Acatl (cane)

Malinalli (herb)

Mexico
Aztec
Day signs

Tecpatl (stone)

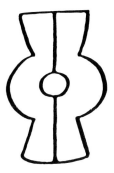

Ollin (movement)

Cozcaquahtl (vulture)

221

Quiauitl (rain)

Xochitl (flower)

Mexico
Aztec
Day signs

222

Mexico
Aztec
Year bearers

Mexico
Aztec
Day 6 serpent in the year 12 rabbit (Date of Birth)

224

Peru
Inca
Cabuya

Mexico
Teotihuacan
Sacrificial heart

Mexico
Teotihuacan
Obsidian sacrificial knives

227

Peru
Bird motif

228

Peru
Serpent

229

Peru
Tiahuanaco
Balsa sign

Peru
Moche
Plants

Mexico
Teotihuacan
Glyphs of the Eye

232

Panama
Beast

233

Mexico
Maya
Death symbol

234

Mexico
Maya
God of Death

235

Mexico
Maya
War God

236

Mexico
Maya
God of human sacrifice

237

Mexico
Maya
Suicide God

238

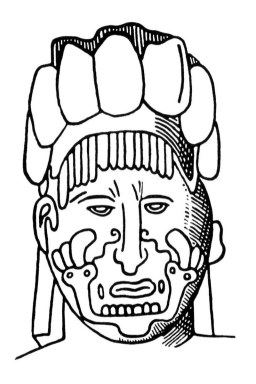

Mexico
Maya
Facial tattoo

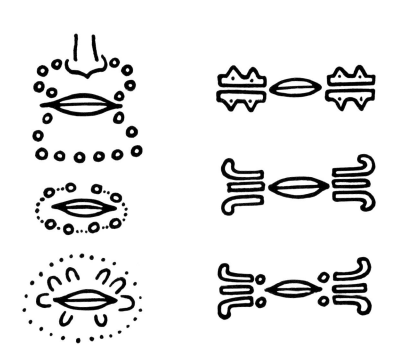

Mexico
Maya
Mouth tattoos

240

Peru
Moche
Snakes

241

Peru
Moche
Fish

242

Peru
Moche
Seabirds

Peru
Moche
Seabirds

244

Peru
Moche
Seabirds

Peru
Moche
Seabirds

Peru
Moche
Seabirds

247

Peru
Moche
Duck

248

Peru
Moche
Deer

Peru
Inca
Bird

250

Peru
Moche
Fish demon

251

Mexico
Aztec
Ocelotl

252

Peru
Inca
Dog

253

Peru
Moche
Feline

254

Peru
Inca
Puma

255

Peru
Moche
Monkey

256

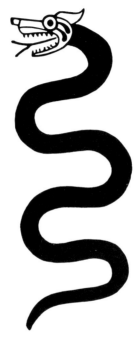

Peru
Snake

Peru
Moche
Octopus

258

Peru
Moche
Fox

259

Peru
Demon

Peru
Moche
Spider

261

Peru
Inca
Lobster

262

Peru
Moche
Dragon

263

Peru
Moche
Sea lion

264

Peru
Moche
Hummingbird

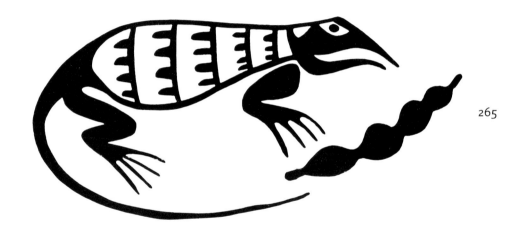

265

Peru
Moche
Lizard

266

Peru
Moche
Barracuda & Bonito

267

Mexico
Totonac
Monkeys

268

Panama
Crocodile

269

Mexico
Totonac
Tattoo designs

270

Panama
Crocodile

Mexico
Aztec
Ugly Earth Toad

272

Mexico
Maya
Bee God

Peru
Inca
Sky animal, feline

274

Peru
Tiahuanaco
Puma

Peru
Inca
Sky animal, feline

Mexico
Serpent

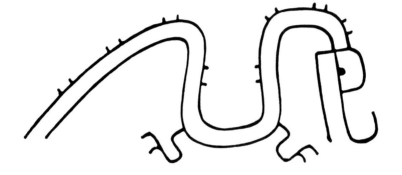

Costa Rica
Crocodile

278

Costa Rica
Crocodile

CAPTIONS

ENGLISH
ESPAÑOL
FRANÇAIS
DEUTSCH
ITALIANO

Page	English	Español

Français	Deutsch	Italiano
Osage-Guerrier avec tatouages de cérémonie	Osage-Krieger mit zeremoniellen Tattoos	Osage-Guerriero con tatuaggi cerimoniali
Mandan-Chef avec symboles de guerre	Mandan-Häuptling mit Kriegssymbolen	Mandan-Capitribù con simboli di guerra
Haida-Homme avec bras et poitrine tatoués	Haida-Mann mit Brust und Arm Tattoos	Haida-Uomo con tatuaggi sul petto e sul braccio
Arapaho-Chef Black Coyote	Arapaho-Häuptling Schwarzer Koyote	Arapaho-Capotribù Black Coyote (Coyote Nero)
Mohawk-Chef Sa Ga Yeath Qua Pieth Tow	Mohawk-Häuptling Sa Ga Yeath Qua Pieth Tow	Mohawk-Capotribù Sa Ga Yeath Qua Pieth Tow
Haida-Homme avec bras et poitrine tatoués	Haida-Mann mit Brust und Arm Tattoos	Haida-Uomo con tatuaggi sul petto e sul braccio
Minitari-Guerrier tatoué	Minitari-Tätowierter Krieger	Minitari-Guerriero tatuato
Kutchin-Guerrier avec des tatouages faciaux	Kutchin-Krieger mit Gesichts-Tattoos	Kutchin-Guerriero con tatuaggi facciali
Dakota-Guerrier tatoué	Dakota-Tätowierter Krieger	Dakota-Guerriero tatuato
Cree-Chef tatoué	Cree-Tätowierter Häuptling	Cree-Capitribù tatuati
Timucua-Chefs	Timucua-Häuptlinge	Timucua-Capitribù
Sioux-Guerrier	Sioux-Krieger	Sioux-Guerriero
Haida-Halibut	Haida-Halibut	Haida-Rombo
Haida-Double oiseau de tonnerre	Haida-Doppelter Donnervogel	Haida-Disegno doppio di Uccello di Tuono
Haida-Poisson Aigle	Haida-Fischadler	Haida-Pesce Aquila
Haida-Tête de baleine	Haida-Walköpfe	Haida-Testa di balena
Inuit-1566	Inuit-1566	Inuit-1566
Chinook-Femme tatouée à tête modifiée	Chinook-Tätowierte Frau mit modifiziertem Kopf	Chinook-Donna tatuata e con testa modificata
Wichita-Femme Tatouée	Wichita-Tätowierte Frau	Wichita-Donna tatuata
Naskapi-Femme avec tatouage de croix chrétienne	Naskapi-Frau mit christl. Kreuz Tattoo	Naskapi-Donna con una croce cristiana tatuata
Mohave-Femme tatouée	Mohave-Tätowierte Frau	Mohave-Donna tatuata
Inuit-Femme tatouée	Inuit-Tätowierte Frau	Inuit-Donna tatuata
Ponca-Fille tatouée	Ponca-Tätowierters Mädchen	Ponca-Ragazza tatuata
Louisiana-Prêtre du soleil	Louisiana-Sonnenpriester	Louisiana-Sacerdote del sole
Haida-Tatoue couple	Haida-Tätowiertes Paar	Haida-Coppia tatuata
Haida-Tatoue couple	Haida-Tätowiertes Paar	Haida-Coppia tatuata
Iroquois-Guerrier tatoué	Iroquois-Tätowierter Krieger	Irochesi-Guerriero tatuato
Osage-Guerrier avec des symboles de guerre	Osage-Krieger mit Kriegssymbolen	Osage-Guerriero con simboli di guerra
Florida-Guerrier tatoué	Florida-Tätowierter Krieger	Florida-Guerriero tatuato
Creek-Guerrier à poitrine tatouée	Creek-Krieger mit Brust-Tattoo	Creek-Guerriero con tatuaggi sul petto
Haida-Oiseau de tonnerre	Haida-Donnervogel	Haida-Uccello di Tuono
Mimbres-Poisson	Mimbres-Fisch	Mimbres-Pesce
Mimbres-Poisson	Mimbres-Fisch	Mimbres-Pesce
Lavantin	Manatee	Manatee
Mimbres-Tortue	Mimbres-Schildkröte	Mimbres-Tartaruga
Motif d'oiseau	Vogelmotiv	Motivo composto da uccelli

Page	English	Español
49	Plains Cree-Buffalo That Walks Like a Man	Plains Cree-Búfalo que camina como un hombre
50	Bird motif	Tema pájaro
51	SW America-Spiral bird motif	SO América-Espiral tema pájaro
52	SW America-Spiral motif	SO América-Espiral tema pájaro
53	NW Coast-Hocker design	NW Coast-Diseño Hocker
54	Tsimshian-Bear	Tsimshian-Oso
55	Haida-Bear	Haida-Oso
56	Haida-Bear	Haida-Oso
57	Haida-Bear	Haida-Oso
58	Haida-Bear cub	Haida-Cachorro de oso
59	Haida-Wasgo (Sea Wolf)	Haida-Wasgo (Lobo de mar)
60	Haida-Wasgo (Sea Wolf)	Haida-Wasgo (Lobo de mar)
61	Haida-Killer Whale	Haida-Ballena asesina
62	NW Coast-Double Killer Whale	Costa NO-Doble ballena asesina
63	Kwakiutl-Killer Whale	Kwakiutl-Ballena asesina
64	Haida-Orca	Haida-Orca
65	Kwakiutl-Whale	Kwakiutl-Ballena
66	Haida-Fabulous Sea Monster	Haida-Monstruo fabuloso del mar
67	Haida-Dogfish	Haida-Perro pescado
68	Haida-Squid	Haida-Calamar
69	Haida-Sculpin	Haida-Sculpin
70	Haida-Sculpin	Haida-Sculpin
71	Haida-Sculpin	Haida-Sculpin
72	Haida-Sculpin	Haida-Sculpin
73	Haida-Sculpin	Haida-Sculpin
74	Haida-Cod	Haida-Bacalao
75	Kwakiutl-Eyes	Kwakiutl-Ojos
76	Kwakiutl-Wing and fin designs	Kwakiutl-Diseños de alas y aletas
77	Kwakiutl-Wing and fin designs	Kwakiutl-Diseños de alas y aletas
78	Kwakiutl-Thunderbird	Kwakiutl-Pájaro de trueno
79	Tlingit-Thunderbird	Tlingit-Pájaro de trueno
80	Kwakiutl-Thunderbird	Kwakiutl-Pájaro de trueno
81	Haida-Thunderbird	Haida-Pájaro de trueno
82	NW America-Eagle	NO-América-Águila
83	Kwakiutl-Thunderbird	Kwakiutl-Pájaro de trueno
84	Kwakiutl-Raven	Kwakiutl-Cuervo
85	Haida-Double Thunderbird	Haida-Doble pájaro de Trueno
86	Haida-Duck	Haida-Pato
87	Haida-Double Raven	Haida-Doble cuervo

Français	Deutsch	Italiano
Cree-Buffle Qui Marche Comme un Homme	Prärie Cree-Büffel, der wie ein Mensch geht	Cree-Bufalo Che Cammina Come un Uomo
Motif Oiseau	Vogelmotiv	Motivo composto da uccelli
Amérique SO-motif spirale oiseau	SW Amerika-Spiral Vogel Motiv	America s-o-Motivo a spirale composto da uccelli
Amérique SO-Motif spirale	SW Amerika-Spiral Motiv	America sud-ovest-Motivo a spirale
-Côte NO-design Hocker	NW Coast-Hocker Design	Costa nord-ovest-Disegno Hocker
Tsimshian-Ours	Tsimshian-Bär	Tsimshian-Orso
Haida-Ours	Haida-Bär	Haida-Orso
Haida-Ours	Haida-Bär	Haida-Orso
Haida-Ours	Haida-Bär	Haida-Orso
Haida-Ourson	Haida-Bärenjunges	Haida-Cucciolo d'Orso
Haida-Wasgo (Loup de mer)	Haida-Wasgo (Seewolf)	Haida-Wasgo (Pescegatto)
Haida-Wasgo (Sea Wolf)	Haida-Wasgo (Seewolf)	Haida-Wasgo (Pescegatto)
Haida-Baleine tueuse	Haida-Killerwal	Haida-Orca Assassina
Côte NO-Double baleine tueuse	NW Küste-Doppelter Killerwal	Costa n-o-Disegno doppio di orca assassina
Kwakiutl-Baleine Tueuse	Kwakiutl-Killerwal	Kwakiutl-Orca assassina
Haida-Orque	Haida-Orca-Wal	Haida-Orca marina
Kwakiutl-Baleine	Kwakiutl-Wal	Kwakiutl-Orca
Haida-Fabuleux monster des mers	Haida-Sagenhaftes Seemonster	Haida-Mostro marino mitologico
Haida-Poisson chien	Haida-Dog-Fisch	Haida -Pescecane
Haida-Calamar	Haida-Tintenfisch	Haida-Seppia
Haida-Sculpin	Haida-Stichling	Haida-Sculpin
Haida-Sculpin	Haida-Stichling	Haida-Sculpin
Haida-Sculpin	Haida-Stichling	Haida-Sculpin
Haida-Sculpin	Haida-Stichling	Haida-Sculpin
Haida-Sculpin	Haida-Stichling	Haida-Sculpin
Haida-Cabillaud	Haida-Hummer	Haida-Merluzzo
Kwakiutl-Yeux	Kwakiutl-Augen	Kwakiutl-Occi
Kwakiutl-designs aile et nageoire	Kwakiutl-Flügel und Flossen Design	Kwakiutl-Disegni di ali e pinne
Kwakiutl-designs aile et nageoire	Kwakiutl-Flügel und Flossen Design	Kwakiutl-Disegni di ali e pinne
Kwakiutl-Oiseau de tonnerre	Kwakiutl-Donnervogel	Kwakiutl-Uccello di Tuono
Tlingit-Oiseau de tonnerre	Tlingit-Donnervogel	Tlingit-Uccello di Tuono
Kwakiutl-Oiseau de tonnerre	Kwakiutl-Donnervogel	Kwakiutl-Uccello di Tuono
Haida-Oiseau de tonnerre	Haida-Donnervogel	Haida-Uccello di Tuono
Amérique du NO-Aigle	NW Amerika-Adler	America nord-ovest-Aquila
Kwakiutl-Oiseau de tonnerre	Kwakiutl-Donnervogel	Kwakiutl-Uccello di Tuono
Kwakiutl-Corbeau	Kwakiutl-Rabe	Kwakiutl-Corvo
Haida-Double Oiseau de tonnerre	Haida-Doppelte Donnervogel	Haida-Disegno doppio di un Uccello di Tuono
Haida-Canard	Haida-Ente	Haida-Anatra
Haida-Double Corbeau	Haida-Doppelter Rabe	Haida-Doppio Corvo

Français	Deutsch	Italiano
Haida-Corbeau	Haida-Rabe	Haida-Corvo
Haida-Corneille	Haida-Krähe	Haida-Corvo
Haida-Double Corbeau	Haida-Doppelter Rabe	Haida-Doppio Corvo
Kwakiutl-Corbeau	Kwakiutl-Rabe	Kwakiutl-Corvo
Haida-Corbeau mythique	Haida-Mystischer Rabe	Haida-Corvo mitologico
Haida-Libellelule	Haida-Libelle	Haida-Libellula
Tsimshian-Libellule	Tsimshian-Libelle	Tsimshian-Libellula
Haida-Mite	Haida-Falke-Motte	Haida-Hawk-moth (lepidottero Sfinge del Galio)
Haida-Grenouille	Haida-Frosch	Haida-Rana
Haida-Ours Grizzly	Haida-Grizzly Bär	Haida-Orso Grizzly
Haida-Chèvre de Montagne	Haida-Bergziege	Haida-Stambecco
Haida-Castor	Haida-Biber	Haida-Castoro
Kwakiutl-Castor	Kwakiutl-Biber	Kwakiutl-Castoro
Haida-Ours et tshimo's	Haida-Bär und tshimo's	Haida-Orso e tshimo's
Haida-Oiseau de tonnerre et tshimo's	Haida-Donnervogel und tshimo's	Haida-Uccello di Tuono e tshimo's
Haida-Oiseau de tonnerre	Haida-Donnervogel	Haida-Uccello di Tuono
Haida-Oiseau de tonnerre	Haida-Donnervogel	Haida-Uccello di Tuono
Haida-Double Loup	Haida-Doppelter Wolf	Haida-Disegno doppio di Lupo
Haida-Bracelet Ours	Haida-Bär-Armband	Haida-Bracciale con orso
Haida-Bracelet Monstre des mers	Haida-Seemonster-Armband	Haida-Braccialetto con mostro marino
Haida-Bracelet Castor	Haida-Biber-Armband	Haida-Braccialetto con castoro
Kwakiutl-Faucon	Kwakiutl-Falke	Kwakiutl-Falco
Tsimshian-Monstre des mers	Tsimshian-Seemonster	Tsimshian-Mostro marino
Kwakiutl-Sisiutl (esprit du serpent)	Kwakiutl-Sisiutl (Schlangengeist)	Kwakiutl-Sisiutl (spirito serpente)
Georgia-Serpent anthropomorphe	Georgia-Vermenschlichte Schlange	Georgia-Serpente antropomorfe
Mohegan-designs Backs	Mohegan-Rücken-Designs	Mohegan-Designs sulla schiena
Osage-tatouage de cérémonie sur poitrine	Osage-Zeremonielles Brust-Tattoo	Osage-Tatuaggio cerimoniale sul petto
Cree des Plaines-Grizzly Ours Grizzly	Prärie Cree-Grizzly Bär	Pianure Cree-Orso Grizzly
Cree-Serpent à sonnette et Esprit de Buffle	Prärie Cree-Klapperschlange und Büffel-Geist	Cree-Serpente a sonagli e spirito del Bufalo
Cree des Plaines-Oiseau de tonnerre bébé	Prärie Cree-Baby Donnervogel	Pianure Cree-Piccolo di Uccello di Tuono
Cree des Plaines-Manitou	Prärie Cree-Manitu	Pianure Cree-Manito
Cree des Plaines-Oiseaux de tonnerre	Prärie Cree-Donnervögel	Pianure Cree-Uccelli di Tuono
Ojibwa-Oiseau de tonnerre	Ojibwa-Donnervogel	Ojibwa-Uccello di Tuono
Ojibwa-Homme squelette et Loutre	Ojibwa-Skelett Mann und Otter	Ojibwa –Scheletro e Lontra
Thompson tatouages	Thompson Tattoo Designs	Disegno di tatuaggio Thompson
Yavapai tatouages	Yavapai Tattoo Designs	Disegno di tatuaggio Yavapai
Plains-Geometrical designs	Prärie-Geometrisch Designs	Pianure-Disegni Geometrici
Yuki-Designs Quailtip	Yuki-Wachtel-Spitzen Designs	Yuki-Disegno Quailtip
Yuki-Designs Quailtip	Yuki-Wachtel-Spitzen Designs	Yuki-Disegno Quailtip

Page	English	Español

Français

Mimbres-motifs géométriques
Kwakiutl-Sun
Iniut-Serpent
Amérique du SO-Squash blossom
Amérique du SO-Swastika
Inuit-Phoque et serpent
Inuit-Phoque
Inuit-Tatouage traditionnel
Arkansas-serpent à cornes
Haida-Loup
Alabama-Serpent ailé

Deutsch

Mimbres-Geometrischel Designs
Kwakiutl-Sonne
Iniut-Schlange
SW Amerika-Kürbisblüte
SW Amerika-Swastika
Inuit-Seehund and Schlange
Inuit-Seehund
Inuit-Traditionelles Tattoo Design
Arkansas-Gehörnte Schlange
Haida-Wolf
Alabama-Geflügelte Schlange

Italiano

Mimbres-Disegni Geometrici
Kwakiutl-Sole
Inuit-Serpente
America sud-ovest-Fiore di Squash
America sud-ovest-Svastica
Inuit-Foca e serpente
Inuit-Foca
Disegn tradizionale per tatuaggio
Arkansas-Vipera Cornuta
Haida-Lupo
Alabama-Serpente alato

Français	Deutsch	Italiano
Mexique-Masque avec tatouages faciaux	Mexiko-Maske mit Gesichts-Tattoos	Messico-Maschera con tatuaggio facciale
Pérou-Nazca-Figurine avec motifs de tatouages	Peru-Nazca-Statuette mit Tattoo Designs	Perú-Nazca-Statuetta con tatuaggi
Pérou-Nazca-Figurine avec motifs de tatouages	Peru-Nazca-Statuette-Tattoo Designs	Perú-Nazca-Statuetta con tatuaggi
Costa Rica-Figurine avec motifs de tatouages	Costa Rica-Statuette mit Tattoo Designs	Costa Rica-Statuetta con tatuaggi
Inca-Poterie avec motifs de tatouages faciaux	Peru-Inca-Keramik mit Gesichts-Tattoo Designs	Inca-Ceramiche con disegno di tatuaggio facciale
Aztèque-Sacrifice au Soleil	Azteken-Sonnenopfer	Aztechi-Sacrificio del Sole
Brésil-Mundrucu	Brasil-Mundrucu	Brasile-Mundrucu
Mexique-Aztèque-Aigle	Mexiko-Azteken-Adler	Messico-Aztechi-Aquila
Mexique-Aztèque-Aigle	Mexiko-Azteken-Adler	Messico-Aztechi-Aquila
Mexique-Aztèque-Aigle	Mexiko-Azteken-Adler	Messico-Aztechi-Aquila
Mexique-Aztèque-Ocomatli (Dieu Singe)	Mexiko-Azteken-Ocomatli (Affengott)	Messico-Aztechi-Ocomatli (Dio Scimmia)
Mexique-Maya-Hibou	Mexiko-Maya-Eule	Messico-Maya-Gufo
Aztèque-Mictlantecuhtli (Dieu de la mort)	Azteken-Mictlantecuhtli (Gott der Toten)	Messico-Aztechi-Mictlantecuhtli (Dio della morte)
Mexique-Aztèque-Plantes hallucinogènes	Mexiko-Azteken-Hallizogene Pflanzen	Messico-Aztechi-Piante allucinogene
Mexique-Aztèque-Jaguar	Mexiko-Azteken-Jaguar	Messico-Aztechi-Giaguaro
Moche-Poterie avec motifs de tatouages faciaux	Moche-Keramik mit Gesichts-Tattoo Designs	Ceramiche con disegno di tatuaggio facciale
Columbia-Figurine avec motifs de tatouages	Columbia-Statuette Tattoo Designs	Colombia-Statuetta con tatuaggi
Brésil-Mundrucu	Brasil-Mundrucu	Brasile-Mundrucu
Brésil-Mundurucu-Instrument pour tatouer	Brasil-Mundurucu-Tattoo-Werkzeug	Brasile-Mundurucu-Strumento per tatuaggi
Brésil-Tupinamba	Brasil-Tupinamba	Brasile-Tupinamba
Mexique-Serpent craint	Mexiko-Gefiederte Schlange	Messico-Serpente Piumato
Mexique-Arbre Crocodile	Mexiko-Krokodil-Baum	Messico-Albero 'Coccodrillo'
Mexique-Oiseau sacré Quetzal	Mexiko-Heiliger Quetzal Vogel	Messico-Uccello Sacro Quetzal
Mexique-Maya-Quetzalcoatl (Serpent à plumes)	Maya-Quetzalcoatl (Gefiederte Schlange)	Messico-Maya-Quetzalcoatl (Serpente Piumato)
Mexique-Aztèque-Lutte Tigre Aigle	Mexiko-Azteken-Tiger Adler Kampf	Messico-Aztechi-Lotta tra Tigre e Aquila
Mexique-Maya-Le serpent divin Kukulcán	Mexiko-Maya-Die göttliche Schlange Kukulcán	Messico-Maya-Il Serpente divino Kukulcán
Mexique-Quetzalcoatl en Dieu du Vent	Mexiko-Quetzalcoatl als Gott des Windes	Messico-Quetzalcoatl come Dio del Vento
Pérou-Moche-Centipède	Peru-Moche-Tausendfüssler	Perú-Moche-Centopiedi
Mexique-Aigle	Mexiko-Adler	Messico-Aquila
Mexique-Toltèque-Aigle	Mexiko-Toltec-Adler	Messico-Toltechi-Aquila
Mexique-Aztèque-Aigle	Mexiko-Azteken-Adler	Messico-Aztechi-Aquila
Mexique-Toltèque-Vulture	Mexiko-Toltec-Geier	Messico-Toltechi-Avvoltoio
Mexique-Teotihuacan-Aigle solaire	Mexiko-Teotihuacan-Sonnen-Adler	Messico-Teotihuacan-Aquila Solare
Aigle Solaire dévorant des coeurs humains	Solar Adler, menschl. Herzen verschlingend	Messico-Aquila Solare che divora cuori umani
Aztèque-Hieroglyphes de l'Eau qui Brûle	Azteken-Hieroglyphen brennenden Wassers	Aztechi-Gereoglifico delle Acque Infuocate
Mexique-Aztèque-Crâne	Mexiko-Azteken-Totenkopf	Messico-Aztechi-Teschio
Mexique-Monstre	Mexiko-Monster	Messico-Mostro
Mexique-Aztèque-Coatlicue (Déesse de la terre)	Mexiko-Azteken-Coatlicue (Erdgöttin)	Messico-Aztechi-Coatlicue (Dea della Terra)

Français	Deutsch	Italiano
Mexique-Teotihuacan-Tigre Oiseau Serpent	Mexiko-Teotihuacan-Tiger Vogel Schlange	Messico-Teotihuacan-Tigre Uccello Serpente
Teotihuacan-Visage symbolisant le 5. Soleil	Teotihuacan-Gesicht, Symbol der 5. Sonne	Teotihuacan-Faccia che simbolizza il Quinto Sole
Mexique-Nahuatl-Main de Dieu	Mexiko-Nahuatl-Hand Gottes	Messico-Nahuatl-Mano di Dio
Mexique-Teotihuacan-Main de Dieu	Mexiko-Teotihuacan-Hand Gottes	Messico-Teotihuacan-Mano di Dio
Mexique-Teotihuacan-Papillons	Mexiko-Teotihuacan-Schmetterlinge	Messico-Teotihuacan-Farfalle
Mexique-Maya-Soleil et étoiles	Mexiko-Maya-Sonne und Sterne	Messico-Maya-Sole e stelle
Mexique-Teotihuacan-Petits animaux	Mexiko-Teotihuacan-Kleine Tierchen	Messico-Teotihuacan-Piccoli animali
Mexique-Olmèque-Dragon	Mexiko-Olmec-Drache	Messico-Olmec-Drago
Mexique-Olmèque-Dragon	Mexiko-Olmec-Drache	Messico-Olmec-Drago
Pérou-Moche-Homme crabe	Peru-Moche-Krabbenmann	Perú-Moche-Uomo-granchio
Pérou-Moche-Crabe anthropomorphe	Peru-Moche-vermenschlichte Krabbe	Perú-Moche-Granchio antropomorfo
Pérou-Moche-Iguane	Peru-Moche-Leguan	Perú-Moche-Iguana
Teotihuacan-Quetzalcoatl en Dieu de l'aube	Quetzalcoatl als Herr der Dämmerung	Quetzalcoatl raffigurato come il Dio dell'Aurora
Mexique-Maya-Nombres	Mexiko-Maya-Zahlen	Messico-Maya-Numeri
Mexique-Maya-Signes-période	Mexiko-Maya-Periodische Zeichen	Messico-Maya-Simboli del Ciclo
Mexique-Maya-Signes-mois (année solaire)	Mexiko-Maya-Monatszeichen	Maya-Simboli del Mese (calendario solare)
Mexique-Maya-Signes-jour	Mexiko-Maya-Tageszeichen	Messico-Maya-Simboli del Giorno
Mexique-Maya-Corps célestes	Mexiko-Maya-Himmelskörper	Messico-Maya-Corpi divini
Mexique-Maya-Corps célestes	Mexiko-Maya-Himmelskörper	Messico-Maya-Corpi divini
Mexique-Maya-Glyphes de mort	Mexiko-Maya-Todeszeichen	Messico-Maya-Simboli di morte
Mexique-Aztèque-Spiderwater (orchidée)	Mexiko-Azteken-Spiderwater (Orchidee)	Messico-Aztec-Spiderwater (orchidea)
Mexique-Serpent	Mexiko-Schlange	Messico-Serpente
Mexique-Oiseau motif	Mexiko-Vogelmotiv	Messico-Motivo composto da uccelli
Pérou-Jaguar	Peru-Jaguar	Perú-Giaguaro
Mexique-Design Hocker	Mexiko-Hocker Design	Messico-Disegno Hocker
Mexique-Design Hocker	Mexiko-Hocker Design	Messico-Disegno Hocker
Mexique-Maya-Symbole de mort	Mexiko-Maya-Todessymbol	Messico-Maya-Simboli di morte
Mexique-Aztèque-Coeur percé	Mexiko-Azteken-durchbortes Herz	Messico-Aztechi-Cuore trafitto
Mexique-Aztèque-Coeur percé	Mexiko-Azteken-durchbortes herz	Messico-Aztechi-Cuore trafitto
Mexique-Croix de Quetzalcóatl	Mexiko-Kreuz von Quetzalcoatl	Messico-Croce di Quetzalcoatl
Mexique-Maya-Hieroglyphes de Vénus	Mexiko-Maya-Hieroglyphen der Venus	Messico-Maya-Gereoglifico di Venere
Mexique-Symboles du mouvement	Mexiko-Symbole für Bewegung	Messico-Simboli del movimento
Mexique-Symbole de l'année	Mexiko-Jahressymbol	Messico-Simboli dell'Anno
Zapotèque-Hieroglyphes de l'Etoile du Matin	Mexiko-Zapotec-Hieroglyphen des Morgensterns	Zapotechi-Gereoglifico della Stella del Mattino
Aztèque-Hieroglyphes de matériaux précieux	Azteken-Hieroglypen aus wertvollen Materialien	Messico-Aztechi-Gereoglifici di materiali preziosi
Mexique-Aztèque-Signes-jour	Mexiko-Azteken-Tageszeichen	Messico-Aztechi-Simboli dei giorni
Mexique-Aztèque Signes-jour	Mexiko-Azteken Tageszeichen	Messico-Aztechi-Simboli dei giorni
Mexique-Aztèque-Signes-jour	Mexiko-Azteken-Tageszeichen	Messico-Aztechi-Simboli dei giorni
Mexique-Aztèque-Signes-jour	Mexiko-Azteken-Tageszeichen	Messico-Aztechi-Simboli dei giorni

Français	Deutsch	Italiano
Mexique-Aztèque-Porteurs d'Année	Mexiko-Azteken-Jahresträger	Messico-Aztechi-Portatori dell'anno
Mexique-Aztèque-Une date de naissance	Mexiko-Azteken-Geburtsdatum	Messico-Aztechi-Una data di nascita
Pérou-Inca-Cabuya	Peru-Inca-Cabuya	Perú-Inca-Cabuya
Mexique-Teotihuacan-Coeur à sacrifice	Mexiko-Teotihuacan-Opferherz	Messico-Teotihuacan-Cuore sacrificale
Teotihuacan-Couteaux obsidiens à sacrifice	Mexiko-Teotihuacan-Obsidianische Opfermesser	Teotihuacan-Coltelli sacrificali fatti di ossidiana
Pérou-Motif d'oiseau	Peru-Vogelmotiv	Perú-Motivo composto da uccelli
Pérou-Serpent	Peru-Schlange	Perú-Serpente
Pérou-Tiahuanaco-Signe Balsa	Peru-Tiahuanaco-Balsa Zeichen	Perú Tiahuanaco-Simbolo Balsa
Pérou-Moche-Plantes	Peru-Moche-Pflanzen	Perú-Moche-Piante
Mexique-Teotihuacan-Glyphes de l'oeil	Mexiko-Teotihuacan-Zeichen des Auges	Messico-Teotihuacan-Simbolo dell'Occhio
Panama-Bêtes	Panama-Bestien	Panama-Bestie
Mexique-Maya-Symbole de mort	Mexiko-Maya-Todessymbol	Messico-Maya-Simbolo di morte
Maya-Dieu de la mort	Mexiko-Maya-Gott des Todes	Maya-Dio della Morte
Maya-Dieu de la guerre	Maya-Kriegsgott	Maya-Dio della Guerra
Maya-Dieu du sacrifice humain	Maya-Gott der Menschenopfer	Maya-Dio dei sacrifici umani
Maya-Dieu du suicide	Maya-Gott des Suizids	Maya-Dio del Suicidio
Mexique-Maya avec tatouages faciaux	Mexiko-Maya mit Gesichts-Tattoos	Messico-Maya withcon tatuaggi facciali
Mexique-Maya-Tatouages de la bouche	Mexiko-Maya-Mund-Tattoos	Messico-Maya-Tatuaggi per bocca
Pérou-Moche-Serpents	Peru-Moche-Schlangen	Perú-Moche-Serpenti
Pérou-Moche-Poisson	Peru-Moche-Fisch	Perú-Moche-Pesce
Pérou-Moche-Oiseaux de mer	Peru-Moche-Seevögel	Perú-Moche-Gabbiani
Pérou-Moche-Oiseaux de mer	Peru-Moche-Seevögel	Perú-Moche-Gabbiani
Pérou-Moche-Oiseaux de mer	Peru-Moche-Seevögel	Perú-Moche-Gabbiani
Pérou-Moche-Oiseaux de mer	Peru-Moche-Seevögel	Perú-Moche-Gabbiani
Pérou-Moche-Oiseaux de mer	Peru-Moche-Seevögel	Perú-Moche-Gabbiani
Pérou-Moche-Canard	Peru-Moche-Ente	Perú-Moche-Anatra
Pérou-Moche-Cerf	Peru-Moche-Wild	Perú-Moche-Cervo
Pérou-Inca-Oiseau	Peru-InKa-Vogel	Perú-Inca-Uccello
Pérou-Poisson démon	Peru-Fisch Dämon	Perú-Pesce demone
Mexique-Aztèque-Ocelotl	Mexiko-Azteken-Ozelot	Messico-Aztechi-Ocelotl
Pérou-Inca-Chien	Peru-Inka-Hund	Perú-Inca-Cane
Pérou-Moche-Félin	Peru-Moche-Katze	Perú-Moche-Felino
Pérou-Inca-Puma	Peru-Inca-Puma	Perú-Inca-Puma
Pérou-Moche-Singe	Peru-Moche-Affe	Perú-Moche-Scimmia
Pérou-Serpent	Peru-Schlange	Perú-Serpente
Pérou-Moche-Pieuvre	Peru-Moche-Octopus	Perú-Moche-Polipo
Pérou-Moche-Renard	Peru-Moche-Fuchs	Perú-Moche-Volpe
Pérou-Démon	Peru-Dämon	Perú-Demone
Pérou-Moche-Araignée	Peru-Moche-Spinne	Perú-Moche-Ragno

Page	English	Español

Français	Deutsch	Italiano
Pérou-Inca-Homard	Peru-Inka-Hummer	Perú-Inca-Aragosta
Pérou-Moche-Dragon	Peru-Moche-Drache	Perú-Moche-Drago
Pérou-Moche-Lion de mer	Peru-Moche-Seelöwe	Perú-Moche-Leone Marino
Pérou-Moche-Colibri	Peru-Moche-Kolibri	Perú-Moche-Colibrí
Pérou-Moche-Lézard	Peru-Moche-Eidechse	Perú-Moche-Lucertola
Pérou-Moche-Barracuda et Bonite	Peru-Moche-Barracuda und Bonito	Perú-Moche-Barracuda e bonito
Mexique-Totonaque-Singes	Mexiko-Totonac-Affen	Messico-Totonachi-Scimmia
Panama-Crocodile	Panama-Krokodil	Panama-Coccodrillo
Mexique-Totonaque-Motifs de tatouages	Mexiko-Totonac-Tattoo Designs	Messico-Totonachi-Disegni
Panama-Crocodile	Panama-Krokodil	Panama-Coccodrillo
Mexique-Aztèque-Vilain Crapaud de Terre	Mexiko-Azteken-Hässliche Erdkröte	Messico-Aztechi-Ugly Earth Toad (Rana)
Mexique-Maya-Dieu Abeille	Mexiko-Maya-Bienengott	Messico-Maya-Dio Ape
Pérou-Inca-Animal du ciel, félin	Peru-Inka-Himmelstiere, Katze	Perú-Inca-Animale celeste, felino
Pérou-Tiahuanaco-Puma	Peru-Tiahuanaco-Puma	Perú-Tiahuanaco-Puma
Pérou-Inca-Animal du ciel, félin	Peru-Inka-Himmelstiere, Katze	Perú-Inca-Animale celeste, felino
Mexique-Serpent	Mexiko-Schlange	Messico-Serpente
Costa Rica-Crocodile	Costa Rica-Krokodil	Costa Rica-Coccodrillo
Costa Rica-Crocodile	Costa Rica-Krokodil	Costa Rica-Coccodrillo